VINCENT
VAN GOGH

Eileen Lucas

Vincent VAN GOGH

A FIRST BOOK 1991
FRANKLIN WATTS
NEW YORK / LONDON / TORONTO / SYDNEY

Frontispiece: Detail from *Pollard Willows and Setting Sun*

Cover photographs courtesy of: The Collection of
Mrs. John Hay Whitney

Photographs courtesy of: Art Resource: pp. 2 (Bridgeman), 8, 26, 39 (all Giraudon), 23 (Albert Moldvay), 27 (Sef), 28, 52, 53, 56 (all Scala), 42; Stedelijk Museum, Amsterdam; pp. 11, 18; The Museum of Fine Arts, Boston: pp. 22 (Arthur G. Tompkins Residuary Fund), 34 (Gift of Robert Treat Paine, 2nd), 50 (Bequest of John T. Spaulding); The Cleveland Museum of Art: p. 32 (Gift of the Hanna Fund); Vincent Van Gogh Foundation/National Museum of Vincent Van Gogh, Amsterdam: p. 36; The Toledo Museum of Art: p. 37; The Museum of Modern Art, N.Y.: pp. 44 (Abby Aldrich Rockefeller Bequest), 45 (Lillie P. Bliss Bequest); The Metropolitan Museum of Art: p. 48 (Gift of Adele R. Levy, 1958. (58, 187) photograph by Malcolm Varon); The National Gallery of Art, Washington: p. 51 (Chester Dale Collection).

Library of Congress Cataloging-in-Publication Data

Lucas, Eileen
Vincent Van Gogh / Eileen Lucas.
p. cm.—(A First book)
Includes bibliographical references and index.
Summary: Briefly examines the life of the renowned Dutch painter
and traces the development of his art.
ISBN 0-531-20024-8
1. Gogh, Vincent Van, 1853–1890—Juvenile literature.
2. Painters—Netherlands—Biography—Juvenile literature.
[1. Gogh, Vincent Van, 1853–1890. 2. Artists. 3. Painting, Dutch.
4. Painting, Modern—19th century—Netherlands. 5. Art
appreciation.] I. Title II. Series.
ND653.G7L755 1991
759.9492—dc20
[B]
[92]

90-47222 CIP AC

CONTENTS

For Mom and Dad, and for Joe.
Thanks for believing in me.

"The sight of stars always sets me dreaming."

—Vincent Van Gogh
1853–1890

THE HAGUE:
"I Want to Succeed"

The grime of the city was the first thing that sixteen-year-old Vincent Van Gogh noticed as he stepped off the train. So many people, all in such a hurry. Well, of course. The Hague was one of the biggest cities in Holland in 1869.

Vincent caught sight of his reflection in a shop window opposite the train station. His mother had taken such care to set his unruly red hair straight before he'd left home, but now it was standing up in all directions. He must have been running his hands through it during the trip—a nervous habit he would have to break now that he was going to work in Uncle Vincent's art gallery. As co-owner of the Goupil galleries, Uncle Vincent was a very successful and important man, and young Vincent wanted very much to be successful too.

Self-portrait, 1889

9

Vincent Van Gogh was born in the small Dutch village of Groot Zundert on March 30, 1853, the first of six children born to Theodorus and Anna Cornelia Van Gogh. His mother was a kind and gentle woman. She loved all of her children very much, even the emotional, argumentative Vincent, who always seemed just a little different from her other children. Vincent's father was the minister of the small community where they lived.

Being the oldest, Vincent was often in charge of the younger children. He enjoyed making up games for them to play, and he was especially fond of his younger brother Theo. He didn't mind when Theo tagged along on the long walks he liked to take. They pretended that these were great adventures, searches for such treasures as abandoned birds' nests, strange mushrooms, and colorful insects.

These things of nature fascinated Vincent. Once he drew a sketch of some of these "treasures," but he became embarrassed when his mother complimented him on it. She liked to draw flowers, and Vincent thought that her work was much better than his.

Several years went by and Vincent learned much in his uncle's art gallery. Some days he worked in the back room, opening and unloading crates of paintings. He loved being near the paintings; he loved to smell them and run his fingers over them when no one was looking. He often discussed these works of art with the clerks in the gallery,

Vincent at age thirteen

giving his opinion of different techniques and styles. He liked to talk about the way different paintings made him feel.

One day his uncle came into the back room to tell Vincent that there was an opening for a clerk in the Goupil art gallery in London. It would be only a small promotion, but at least it would get Vincent out of the back room. At the age of twenty, Vincent was going to London! He was sure that this would be his big chance to prove himself to his family and to the world.

THE BORINAGE:
"I Want to Serve"

At first, things went well for Vincent in London. He was fascinated with British art and literature, and he enjoyed being in England. Then he fell in love with his landlady's daughter, which seemed a wonderful thing to him, but she was engaged to another man.

Vincent was so upset by this that he became impossible to get along with at work. Soon he quit his job, but he wasn't sure what he wanted to do next. He traveled back and forth between Holland, England, and France for several years, trying to find a place and a career that was right for him.

One of the things Vincent tried was preaching. He found that he enjoyed it. So he decided to follow in his father's footsteps and become a minister.

In 1877, at the age of twenty-four, Vincent went to

Amsterdam to study for the ministry. He didn't do well at the university, though, so he went to Brussels, Belgium, to study at a small school. This was considered to be a step down by his family, since an evangelist from a small school would only be able to minister to the poor. A university graduate could be responsible for a well-to-do community. But Vincent knew in his heart that he did not belong among the well-to-do.

Then he failed at the evangelist school too. Fortunately, one of his teachers offered him a position as lay preacher in the Borinage, a very poor coal-mining region in the south of Belgium. It wasn't much of a position, but at least it was a start.

The whistle of the train pulling into the station woke Vincent from a daydream. He'd been thinking about the past again. Enough of that. Here he was in the Borinage, his new home. Now that the way had been opened for him to preach, something he thought he could do and do well, he vowed to himself that he would not fail at this. He was twenty-five years old, and it was time he got settled into something.

Quickly, he gathered his few belongings and got off the train. He looked around the bleak countryside and then headed for the home of Madame Denis, who had offered to board the new preacher. Hers was the only brick home in the miners' village. The rest of the community was made up of small, one-room shacks with coal-burning stoves in the center and a few belongings scattered around.

The miners worked in the coal mines six days a week, from before sunup to after sundown. The mines were dirty and dangerous; yet the workers earned barely enough to keep from starving in return for their labor.

On Sunday mornings they packed the shed behind the bakery where Vincent held services. As he looked out at their coal-blackened faces, Vincent struggled to find just the right words to give them hope and comfort. Never before had he felt so needed, and more than anything else, Vincent wanted to be needed.

There was hardly a household that was not touched by his goodness. His natural generosity led him to give whatever the people needed most—a loaf of bread to one family, a burlap sack to block the cold wind from coming through the cracks in the home of another. He nursed the sick and played with the children.

Vincent moved into a shack that was in even worse condition than most of the miners', because he didn't feel right sleeping in his comfortable room in Mrs. Denis's big, warm house in the midst of such poverty. He gave away all his clothes except the ones on his back and ate only the hard bread and cheese that the miners ate. As a result, he even shared their illnesses, suffering from almost constant fever and malnutrition.

It became harder and harder for Vincent to find words

of hope on Sunday mornings. He felt bad that he could not improve conditions for the miners.

And then the committee that had given Vincent permission to preach to the miners fired him. He had written to them asking for more help for the miners. They not only did not send help, they let him know that they did not approve of the way in which he was living.

Vincent stopped preaching, but he did not leave the Borinage. He filled his days sketching pictures of the people around him. They were not very good, he would admit, but still they seemed to capture something of the spirit of the people. He knew their suffering because it had been his suffering too, and this showed in his drawings.

Sketching was Vincent's only comfort, and he devoted himself to it. He simply let time go by without making any decisions until finally one day his brother Theo arrived.

3 THE HAGUE, AGAIN: "I Want to Draw"

Vincent's family had sent Theo to the Borinage, hoping that Theo could talk some sense into Vincent, to convince him to come home and decide what to do with his life. Theo just wanted to see what his brother was doing, to see if he was happy.

As he gazed upon his older brother lying ill and hungry in the small, hard bed, Theo realized how much he cared about him. He was upset to see how Vincent was living; there weren't even any sheets on the bed! Theo was now a successful art dealer in the Goupil gallery in Paris. He liked to dress well and lived in a comfortable, well-furnished apartment. He wasn't rich, but he lived the life of a gentleman.

During Theo's visit, the brothers talked about their childhood and about the future. Vincent showed Theo his

Vincent had a very close relationship with
his brother Theo. Throughout Van Gogh's
troubled life, Theo always stood by him
and was a source of great comfort.

drawings, and together they decided that Vincent should be an artist. Theo gave Vincent some money so that he could get started. He agreed to send a monthly allowance until Vincent could support himself.

Before they parted, the brothers promised each other that they would never let distance come between them again. For the rest of their lives, the two Van Gogh brothers wrote long and frequent letters to each other, sharing their thoughts about all that mattered in their lives.

After spending some time at his parents' home, Vincent returned to the Hague, where he had once worked in his uncle's gallery. He set up a studio and put all his efforts into his new profession. Each month Theo would send him what money he could so that Vincent could buy art supplies and pay models, pay the rent, and buy food—in that order. If the money ran out before he bought food, Vincent didn't eat.

What frustrated Vincent most was not having money for art supplies. He believed that as long as he could sketch and paint he was getting closer to success. When he had to sit in his studio and wait for money to arrive from Theo, he would begin to get discouraged. To combat this, he would take long walks, getting inspiration from nature.

He wrote long letters to Theo, pouring out his heart and soul:

Dear Theo,

I feel a power in me which I must develop, a fire that I may not quench, but must keep ablaze though I do not know where it will lead me to.

Another time he wrote:

Dear Theo,

When starting out, one makes it very hard on oneself, by a feeling of not being able to master the work . . . by a lack of self-confidence. This cannot be helped, and is a time which one must go through. . . . In my opinion, I am rich because I have found in my work something which I can devote myself to and which inspires me and gives meaning to life.

With a handshake,
yours,
Vincent

While in the Hague, Vincent cared for a woman who had led a very hard life. He painted a picture of her which he called *Sorrow.* He was pleased that it seemed truthful about the life of struggle and hardship that she had.

Struggle was something that Vincent knew a lot about. He struggled to express himself and could not understand why no one saw what he saw in his art, why no one wanted to buy his work. An uncle, Cornelius Van Gogh, bought a few of Vincent's drawings and said that he would buy more if Vincent could only make some "pretty" things. But Vincent wasn't interested in "pretty" things. He went on painting as his heart told him to.

Vincent's bad temper and unconventional behavior made it difficult for him to get along with people who might have been able to help him. A friend who was a painter and another who was an art dealer visited Vincent in his studio frequently for a while. Eventually, both got tired of quarreling with him and they refused to have anything to do with him anymore.

Vincent was often very sick while in the Hague. At one point, he thought he was dying. Only Theo's support and his own belief that he was meant to be a painter kept him going.

In December of 1883, at the age of thirty, Vincent left the Hague. After spending some time with his parents, he moved in with some peasant families in the small Dutch town of Nuenen. There, he continued to sketch the common people: the laborers in the fields, the poor in their homes. For Vincent, it was not enough to draw a peasant; he insisted on drawing peasants at work. This was truth. He wanted people to smell the sweat on the workers when they looked at his paintings.

Slowly but surely, Vincent's care at studying detail and learning the basics was beginning to pay off. He was begin-

(Above) *The Weaver*, 1884
(Facing page) *Peasant Woman*, 1885

ning to feel better about being able to capture what he saw and felt. "I no longer stand helpless before nature as I used to do," he wrote.

After years of studying and sketching peasant hands and faces, Vincent put it all together in a painting called *Five Persons at a Meal*, now commonly known as *The Potato Eaters*. Vincent did not try to make these people beautiful, for they were poor and hardworking, and there was little of beauty in their lives. The painting is dark and eerie and captures the feel of a peasant cottage at dusk as well as the difficult life of its inhabitants. Although now considered one of Van Gogh's masterpieces, no one but Theo seemed to appreciate it much at the time.

Vincent had learned so much about painting already, but he was eager to learn more. Theo told him that there was exciting work being done by painters in Paris. Vincent wanted to see this for himself, so once again he packed his bags and boarded a train, this time headed for Paris.

PARIS:
"I Want to Paint Like Them"

Vincent gazed in awe at the paintings that hung in the Goupil gallery where Theo worked. Theo was helping to promote the work of a group of painters known as Impressionists. Vincent wanted to meet them. He liked the way they used color and light to create "impressions" of what they saw.

Theo introduced Vincent to many of the painters who were working in Paris at this time. Some were Impressionists and some were not. Most were experimenting with new styles of art, and Vincent studied their techniques. He practiced the short, slashing brushstrokes used by some of his friends and the dots of color used by others. He painted portraits of himself and others, flower studies, and bright landscapes. Like a butterfly emerging from a cocoon, the great wealth of creative ability that had been locked up

(Above) *Le moulin de la Galette*, 1886
(Facing page) *Fritillaires*, 1886

inside of Vincent was now released. The drive to express himself had always been there. The tools he needed, color and light, were finally his.

This was a happy time for Vincent. With all that he was learning and the excitement of Paris, it was good to be alive. Theo, worried about Vincent's poor physical health, sent him to a doctor and a dentist, and tried to see to it that Vincent ate well. Although he was four years younger than Vincent, Theo often acted like a protective older brother.

After Vincent had been staying with him for a few months, Theo wrote a letter to their mother full of optimism and hope. "You would not recognize Vincent, he has changed so much," he wrote. "He is making tremendous progress in his work and is beginning to succeed. He is far more cheerful than before, and is very well liked. . . . If we can keep it up, then I think he has the worst behind him and is going to come out on top."

Unfortunately, this happy time did not last very long. Soon Vincent's peculiar and difficult personality would begin to upset the people around him once again. He became very hard to get along with, arguing with and shouting at everyone, even Theo.

To his sister Wilhelmina, Theo wrote: "It is as if he has two persons in him—one marvelously gifted, delicate and tender, the other egotistical and hardhearted. It is a pity that he is his own enemy, for he makes life difficult not only for others, but for himself."

Vincent knew that he would have to leave Paris. He had learned much about light and color, but he was still struggling to perfect a style that would be all his own. And while he enjoyed the excitement of life in Paris, it was ruining his mental and physical health, and straining his relationship with Theo. Vincent needed to move away from all the others, so that he could find himself.

ARLES:
"I Belong Here"

Vincent next went to Arles, a small town in southern France. Here the sun shone brightly and gave him hope that he would finally find the success which always seemed just beyond his reach.

Each morning Vincent rose at dawn and headed out to paint. Some days he would go to the plum fields and paint the movement of the wind in the trees. Another day, he might paint the farmers plowing their fields under the blazing sun, or he might head for the banks of the Rhone River to paint washerwomen cleaning clothes on rocks in the water.

"Here I see everything in a new way," Vincent wrote to Theo. He was excited by the brilliant colors of the countryside around him and wanted to paint everything he saw. On days when the vicious wind called the mistral blew so

The Road Menders at St.-Rémy, 1889

hard it knocked down his easel, Vincent knelt on his knees and continued to paint with his canvas on the ground. Sometimes he stuck candles in the brim of his hat and went out at night to paint. Not even darkness could stop him from working!

He painted quickly, often completing a canvas in one day. Between February and December of 1888, Vincent completed over ninety drawings and one hundred paintings.

His colors seemed to get lighter and brighter until it almost seemed he was capturing the sun itself. Vincent was very interested in the sun, and yellow became his favorite color. The sun or symbols of it (stars, lanterns, flames, sunflowers) appear in many of his paintings.

Although Vincent liked Arles, most of the people of this small town did not much care for him. With his wild, uncombed red hair, his worn, wrinkled clothes looking as if he'd thrown them on in a hurry in the dark (which, chances are, he had), and his sunburned face, he must have looked a sight. Seeing him dashing about with easel and canvases strapped to his back, the Arlesians took to calling him "Fou-Roux," crazy redhead.

But Vincent didn't pay much attention to the towns-people, and he *had* made one good friend since coming to Arles. Joseph Roulin, the post office official, liked Vincent, and invited him to dinner often. Roulin's wife would fuss over Vincent and see that he ate well while the post-

man listened as the painter lectured excitedly about his theories of art.

Roulin helped Vincent find a house to rent, a yellow house where Vincent could paint to his heart's content. Then Vincent decided to invite other artists to come and paint in the yellow house with him.

First he invited Paul Gauguin, an artist whom he'd met in Paris. Like Vincent, Gauguin was very poor, so Vincent asked Theo for the money to send Paul to Arles.

In October 1888, Theo bought some of Gauguin's work so that the artist could go to Arles. Theo also promised to send Gauguin a monthly allowance, just as he did for Vincent, in return for some additional paintings.

But Vincent had been working too hard in the hot sun and was not well, either physically or mentally. "I must beware of my nerves," he wrote to Theo. Adding someone like Gauguin to the picture at this stage of Vincent's life was like touching a match to a fuse—there was sure to be an explosion.

Paul Gauguin was a very domineering, egotistical, and self-confident man. He undertook to "straighten" Vincent out and teach him just what was what. Vincent was eager to learn, and during Gauguin's first few weeks in Arles, the men often painted together and discussed art and life.

Try as he might, however, Vincent had never been a very good student, and Paul's lectures became less and less welcome. Discussions gave way to heated debates, which

Postman Joseph Roulin, 1888

The Yellow House in Arles, 1888

Wheatfields, 1888

soon turned to violent quarrels. Each man exhausted himself trying to change the other.

Soon both painters' nerves were stretched to the breaking point. By December, Gauguin had decided to leave. Being much larger and stronger, he was afraid that he might hurt Vincent if he became angry enough. Gauguin told his friend that he was going to leave the yellow house and return to Paris.

Vincent begged and cried, trying to convince Gauguin to stay. But Paul's mind was made up, and to get away from Vincent's nagging, he went to stay at an inn.

Vincent felt empty and alone. What he did not realize was that he was very sick and needed help. His highly nervous personality had been pushed beyond its limits. To make matters worse, Vincent was suffering from the effects of sunstroke and other illnesses.

The artist was not thinking straight. He followed Gauguin and attacked him, but the larger man was able to calm Vincent enough to send him back into the house. There, Vincent had a seizure and, while in a trancelike state, took his shaving razor and cut off his ear. The next morning, he was found lying in bed, blood-soaked towels wrapped around his head.

Vincent was taken to a hospital where a kind and sympathetic doctor looked after him. Gauguin sent for Theo and then prepared to return to Paris.

Theo was very upset to see his brother in such terrible

Bedroom at Arles, 1888

mental and physical health. He was afraid that Vincent would not recover. But he had some good news for him. Theo told Vincent that he had met a Dutch girl named Johanna and that he was going to be married. Vincent was happy that at least one of them had found love.

Vincent stayed in the hospital for a while, regaining his health. Theo returned to Paris, but Roulin and some other friends visited Vincent occasionally. When Vincent's head had healed, the doctor, whose name was Rey, told him that he would be released, but he must try to avoid too much excitement, eat well, stay away from alcohol, and always wear a hat in the sun.

Vincent did indeed feel better. He felt so good that he started painting again. Two paintings that he completed between January and March 1889 (*Self-Portrait with Bandaged Ear* and a portrait of Roulin's wife) are just as fine as works he had done the previous year.

Soon, however, Vincent returned to his old ways, forgetting Dr. Rey's advice. Painting in the sun all day without a hat on his head, he had several fits of temper and was finally taken to jail. The Arlesians were afraid of him.

ST.-REMY:
"I Want to Get Well"

The temptation to give up must surely have been strong. But even after all these troubles, Vincent's spirit was not broken. From his jail cell he wrote to Theo, making fun of his problems and telling Theo not to worry about him.

Vincent was allowed to leave the jail, but he was not sure that he could live on his own. His doctor recommended that he check into a sanatorium for a while. He said there was no way of knowing when the fits would occur, and in a sanatorium, there would be people around to care for him.

Vincent wanted very much to conquer his illness. On May 8, 1889, he voluntarily entered the St. Paul sanatorium at St.-Rémy, not very far from Arles. It was set in a quiet and beautiful area, and at first Vincent was fairly

happy there. His seizures seemed to get worse, but he hoped to learn how to control them.

The doctor in charge of the sanatorium allowed Vincent to use an empty room as a studio so that he could paint. He was even allowed to go outside sometimes to paint the countryside around St.-Rémy. The anxiety that Vincent was feeling at this time shows up in some of these paintings, but they are considered great works of art.

In fact, it was during this time, in June 1889, that Vincent painted one of his greatest works, *Starry Night.* Using beautiful blues and yellows, he paints a story of a quiet village and a night come alive with blazing, swirling stars. It is a painting that shows the power of an artist who can take paint and canvas and bring a landscape to life.

Time went on. Vincent painted as much as he could despite the terrible attacks he experienced. During these times, he did not know who or where he was, and the attacks left him completely exhausted. As fall turned into winter, and winter into spring, Vincent began to think more and more about getting out of the sanatorium, but he wasn't sure where he could go. He was terribly afraid of having an attack somewhere where there'd be no one to look after him.

Theo had the perfect solution to the problem. He knew of a doctor who took a special interest in painters. Dr. Gachet was very impressed with Vincent's work and assured

Saint Jean Hospital in St.-Rémy, 1889

(Facing page) *Hospital Corridor at St.-Rémy*, 1889
(Above) *Starry Night*, 1889

Theo that he understood Vincent's illness. The doctor would find a place for Vincent to live near him in Auvers, just outside of Paris. That way, Vincent could live on his own, but the doctor would be there to care for him when the attacks came.

Theo was happy that Vincent seemed to want to get on with life again. Theo's wife, Johanna, had just had a baby boy, and they named him Vincent. A painter named Anna Boch had just bought a painting of Vincent's at a public sale in Belgium. And a critic in Paris had had good things to say about Vincent's work. Perhaps things were looking up for the brothers Van Gogh.

For his part, Vincent was too worn out from illness to appreciate what seemed to be the approach of success. All he wanted now was to paint in peace and to see Theo and his family.

On May 16, 1890, Vincent left St.-Rémy and went to Paris. He spent a few days with Theo, Johanna, and baby Vincent, and visited some of his friends in Paris. Then he went to Auvers to meet Dr. Gachet. It was to be his last move in a life that had taken him so many places in search of happiness.

AUVERS:
"I Am Done"

D r. Gachet's house was easy to find: it was the largest one on the street. Dogs and cats, pigeons and peacocks, wandered about the front yard.

"The good doctor is almost as peculiar as I," Vincent wrote to Theo. But the two men got along fine, and Vincent began to paint again.

Dr. Gachet tried to help Vincent, but the artist was losing touch with reality. The anxieties that he felt are reflected in his paintings of this period. Other artists who had stayed with Dr. Gachet captured the peaceful charm of the nearby village and countryside, while Vincent's paintings were wild and violent, though still beautiful.

Despite his failing health, however, Vincent pushed himself harder and harder, producing more than seventy pictures in two months. He painted everything around

Irises, 1890

him: houses and churches, gardens and fields, and several wonderful portraits of Dr. Gachet.

One Sunday in June, Theo's family came to visit Vincent. They had a picnic lunch at Dr. Gachet's, and Vincent carried the baby around, showing him all the animals.

It would be their last happy time together, for several weeks later, Vincent learned that Theo was having trouble at work and the baby was ill. Theo's trouble at work meant financial difficulty for everyone, and Vincent was afraid that he was too much of a burden for his brother. He felt sad, lonely, and anxious. It was more than a man in Vincent's condition could handle. He painted one of his last paintings, *Crows in the Wheatfield*s, and the distress he was feeling is obvious.

One day Vincent found himself standing in Dr. Gachet's house with a gun in his hand. How did it get there? What was he supposed to do with it? Even in his illness, a voice deep inside him said that he did not want to hurt anyone else. He went home.

The next day Vincent found himself in a field, alone except for the screeching blackbirds, again with the gun in his hand. This time, he shot himself.

Somehow Vincent made it back home. When they found him, Vincent lay unconscious on his bed. He had lost a great deal of blood and his heartbeat was very weak, but he was still alive. Dr. Gachet sent for Theo.

Theo knelt by Vincent's bed, tears streaming down his

(Above) *Houses at Auvers*, 1890
(Facing page) *Girl in White*, 1890

(Above) *Memory of the Garden at Etten*, 1888
(Facing page) *Portrait of Dr. Gachet*, 1890

cheeks. He held his brother's hand. The brothers talked quietly all that day and into the night. Early in the morning, July 29, 1890, Vincent said, "I wish I could go home now," and then he died. He was thirty-seven years old.

A few of Vincent's friends came from Paris for the funeral. They tacked his paintings up on the wall of the room where his body lay. They put bunches of sunflowers on top of his coffin. Theo, Dr. Gachet, and the others wept.

Theo was heartbroken. He never recovered from Vincent's death, and six months later he too died. Theo's wife understood how much the brothers had cared for each other. She saw to it that they were buried next to each other so that they would never be separated again.

EPILOGUE

Many people have speculated as to the exact illness from which Vincent Van Gogh suffered. It is not so important to give his illness a name as it is to understand that he was sick throughout most of his adult life, that many factors combined to make it hard for him to be happy, and that despite all this, he struggled to remain in control and express the feelings in his heart and soul through painting.

Vincent Van Gogh taught us a great deal through his life and his work. He taught us that what matters is to be true to yourself. He worked very hard to make something of his life, struggling against hardship and continuing to pick himself up after each setback.

Vincent Van Gogh spent his life reaching for the stars, always trying desperately to reach what was just beyond his grasp. The stars, like the sun and all its symbols, represent light, and light is hope. Vincent Van Gogh was a man of hope, and that is the message that he left for us.

The Siesta, 1890

MASTERPIECES OF VINCENT VAN GOGH

Between the completion of his first major painting in 1885 and his death in 1890, Vincent Van Gogh produced hundreds of paintings and many more drawings and sketches. Among his most famous works are:

The Potato Eaters (May 1885)
Père Tanguy (1887)
Windmill on Montmartre (1887)
Self-Portrait (Paris) (1887)
Peach Trees in Blossom (April 1888)
The Sower (June 1888)
The Harvest (June 1888)
Sunflowers (August 1888)
Postman Joseph Roulin (August 1888)
Café at Night (September 1888)

The Night Café (September 1888)
Self-Portrait (Arles) (1888)
Bedroom at Arles (October 1889)
Van Gogh's Chair (December 1888)
Gauguin's Chair (December 1888)
Self-Portrait with Bandaged Ear (Spring 1889)
La Berceuse (Spring 1889)
Wheatfield and Cypress Trees (1889)
Starry Night (June 1889)
Self-Portrait (St.-Rémy/Auvers) (1889/1890)
The Church at Auvers (June 1890)
Portrait of Dr. Gachet (June 1890)
Crows in the Wheatfields (July 1890)

FOR FURTHER READING

For Younger Readers (grades 1 and up)
Peter, Adeline, and Ernest Raboff. *Vincent Van Gogh* (An Art for Children Book). Garden City, NY: Doubleday & Co., Inc.
Venezia, Mike. *Van Gogh.* (Getting to Know the World's Greatest Artists Series). Chicago: Children's Press, 1988.

For Intermediate Readers (grades 3 and up)
Measham, Terry. *Van Gogh and His World.* Englewood Cliffs, NJ: Silver Burdett Press, 1980.

For Older Readers (grades 5 and up)
Bernard, Bruce, ed. *Vincent, by Himself.* Boston: Little, Brown & Co., 1985.

Bitossi, Sergio. *Vincent Van Gogh.* (Why They Became Famous Series). Englewood Cliffs, NJ: Silver Burdett Press, 1987.

Hammacher, Abraham. *Van Gogh.* London: Paul Hamlyn Ltd., 1961.

Hillyer, V.M., and E.G. Huey. *Fine Art: The Last Two Hundred Years.* (A Young People's Story of Our Heritage Book). NY: Meredith Press, 1966.

INDEX

Page numbers in *italics* indicate illustrations.

ABOUT THE AUTHOR

Eileen Lucas is a free-lance writer of books for young people and magazine articles. She studied communications in college, and is now busy "communicating" about things she cares about through her writing. She is especially interested in history, peace, creativity, and learning. "I love to learn," she says, and encourages young people to read and learn as much as possible. She lives in south-eastern Wisconsin with her husband and sons, Travis and Brendan.

B
GOGH

Lucas, Eileen Copy 1

Vincent Van Gogh

$11.90

FEB 1 3 1992	DATE		
FEB 2 8 1992			